D0713135

Pet Dogs

Julia Barnes

GARETH**STEVENS**
PUBLISHING
A Member of the WRC Media Family of Companies

Please visit our web site at: www.garethstevens.com
For a free color catalog describing Gareth Stevens Publishing's
list of high-quality books and multimedia programs, call
1-800-542-2595.

Library of Congress Cataloging-in-Publication Data

Barnes, Julia, 1955-
  Pet dogs / Julia Barnes — North American ed.
    p. cm. — (Pet pals)
  Includes bibliographical references and index.
  ISBN-10: 0-8368-6777-7
  ISBN-13: 978-0-8368-6777-0 (lib. bdg.)
  1. Dogs—Juvenile literature. I. Title.
  SF426.5.B3765   2007
  636.7—dc22   2006042378

This edition first published in 2007 by
Gareth Stevens Publishing
A Weekly Reader Company
200 First Stamford Place
Stamford, CT 06912 USA

This U.S. edition copyright © 2007 by Gareth Stevens, Inc.
Original edition copyright © 2007 by Westline Publishing,
P.O. Box 8, Lydney, Gloucestershire, GL15 6YD, United Kingdom.
Additional end matter copyright © 2007 by Gareth Stevens, Inc.

Gareth Stevens series editor: Leifa Butrick
Gareth Stevens cover design: Dave Kowalski
Gareth Stevens art direction: Tammy West

Picture Credits:
Comstock, cover; Warren Photographic, pp. 24, 25 (Jane Burton).
All other images copyright © 2007 by Westline Publishing.

Printed in the United States of America

2 3 4 5 6 7 8 9 10 09 08 07

Cover: Children and puppies make friends easily.

of a pack form close ties with each other. Because they all know their places within their packs, wolves do not waste time or energy fighting with each other. Survival depends on each pack member **cooperating**.

Pack Leaders

A wolf pack has a male leader. He is strong and fit and makes all the decisions for the pack, such as when to go hunting or when to move to a new home. He may have one or two assistants, usually younger wolves, that carry out his orders.

The male leader of the wolf pack mates with the strongest, fittest female in the pack. All the other females obey her. The female leader will be the only one in the pack to produce pups, but all members of the pack will help raise them. Wolves have only one litter of pups a year. The pups' parents are the strongest wolves in the pack, and the pack's pups get the best food, so wolf pups have a good chance of surviving.

It is easy to see a family likeness between this wolf and the dogs people keep as pets.

The Human Bond

Wolves were successful hunters in the wild. Why did they give up their freedom to live with people?

Some twelve thousand years ago, people started to live in permanent homes instead of wandering from place to place. No one knows just how or why wolves came to live with people, but it is possible to make some guesses.

Forming a Partnership

Wolves probably visited human settlements, where they smelled human food, and possibly stole leftovers. Perhaps they warmed themselves by the embers of people's fires. Wolf pups might have made friends with human children. The first wolf to live with people could have been the result of a child asking, "Please Mom, can we keep one?"

When an animal is raised with people, it usually becomes tame. Eventually, the wolf pups that first came to live with people had pups of their own. These pups never knew life in the wild so they would have been even tamer than their parents. These animals then found ways to fit in with people, such as guarding their homes and helping with their hunts.

Pups were probably the first wolves to join the human family circle.

Over time, dogs developed skills that were useful to humans, such as herding livestock.

Domestic Dogs

Wolves developed into **domestic** dogs that lived entirely with people. At first, dogs had many different jobs. Later, people realized that, by **breeding** dogs with particular skills, they could produce animals with all the qualities needed for certain jobs. Specialist breeds were even more useful than ordinary dogs.

- If people wanted good guard dogs, they bred the biggest dogs with the best hearing and the loudest barks.
- If people wanted a dog to **track** animals, they would mate dogs that had the best sense of smell.

- When people started to keep sheep and cattle, they used dogs that were best at creeping up on prey to round up their herds.

Dog breeds began by producing animals with specific skills to perform specific work. Now there are hundreds of different dog breeds.

Paw Mark

When wolves first lived with humans, the people and animals probably huddled together on cold nights and gave each other warmth and comfort. The animals probably greeted family members when they returned home — just like dogs do today.

Perfect Pets

Dogs are among the most popular pets in the world. Forty million households in the United States have dogs.

Dogs are intelligent, loving, and loyal. Dogs fit well into many families. A dog sees its human family as its own special pack, and it is ready to accept the rules laid down by the family "pack leader."

A dog quickly learns its place in the family "pack."

Natural Companions

No other animal is such a perfect companion for people. Dogs make great pets for many reasons.

- Dogs come in all shapes and sizes, so finding just the right fit for almost any home or family is easy.
- Dogs become devoted to their human families and know just how to give love to people who need it.
- Dogs will guard homes and warn their owners when strangers are approaching.
- Dogs need exercising regularly, which is also good for their owners.

- Since dogs can be trained, they can go to many different places with their owners and be part of their owners' lives.
- If owners enjoy training, they can take part, together with their dogs, in many sports, such as agility and competitive obedience.

Owners' Duties

Dogs give their owners love and loyalty. In return, owners must look after their dogs properly.

- Owners must provide well-balanced diets.
- Owners must walk their dogs every day, even in rainy or cold weather.
- Owners need to spend time training their dogs.
- Owners should not leave their dogs alone for long periods. If everyone in a family is usually gone all day, the family should choose a different pet.
- Owners must groom their dogs. Grooming can mean lengthy, daily sessions for long-haired breeds or paying for the services of professional groomers.

Allergy Alert

Some people are **allergic** to dogs and may suffer from skin problems, breathing problems, or watery eyes when dogs are around. Doctors can test to see if a person has this type of allergy before he or she decides to get a dog.

- Owners must provide routine health care for their dogs.
- When owners go away for more than a day and cannot take their dogs along, they must find someone to care for their dogs.

Agility competitions are fun for both dogs and owners.

A Dog's Body

Dogs look different from each other, but their bodies function in the same ways.

Nose
A dog has an amazing sense of smell — about one thousand times better than a human's.

Teeth
An adult dog has forty-two teeth that are perfectly designed for eating meat.

Tongue
A dog does not sweat to cool off the way people do. It holds its tongue out and pants. Panting draws cold air over the dog's tongue and increases **evaporation** in the dog's air passages, which reduces the dog's body heat.

Ears

Depending on the breed, a dog's ears may be erect or semi-erect or lie close to the sides of the dog's head. Dogs have much better hearing than people. They can hear sounds that are four times further away than the sounds people hear. Dogs can use one ear at a time or both ears together.

Eyes

A dog is good at seeing the slightest movement, but it is not so good at seeing objects that are not moving. At night, dogs can see better than people. Dogs see in shades of blues and yellows.

Tail

A dog uses its tail to balance when it is turning corners and moving quickly. A dog also uses its tail to signal other dogs.

Coat

Dogs have many different types of coats. Their coats may be short-haired, long-haired, wire-haired, curly-haired, or even hairless, depending on the breed.

Feet

The underside of a dog's feet have tough, protective pads of skin so the dog can walk on all types of surfaces and withstand heat and cold.

Dog Breeds

More than four hundred different breeds of dogs live all over the world. They all descended from one animal — the wolf.

Dog breeds came about so people could have the best dog for a job that needed to be done. Many dogs still show the working behaviors of their breeds, even though they have never worked.

In the United States, the American Kennel Club (AKC) places every dog breed into one of seven categories, or groups.

Labrador retrievers like to be included in family activities.

Sporting

This category includes the kinds of dogs that were bred for hunting expeditions. Retrievers, spaniels, pointers, and setters each had a different job on the hunting field. Besides being great companions, many of these breeds still work as hunting dogs.

Sporting dogs are athletic and full of energy. They need lots of exercise. They like to work closely with their owners, and they are easy to train. Most sporting dogs make great family pets. Labrador retrievers are the most popular dogs of all breeds in the United States.

Terriers

Terriers are the tough characters of the dog world. Many of the terrier breeds, including Jack Russell terriers, West Highland

Like many small terriers, West Highland white terriers are quick thinkers.

whites, and border terriers, were sent down holes to flush out foxes. These dogs are quick-thinking and determined — and still like to disappear down holes! Many terriers are wire-haired and have coats that do not shed. Terrier's coats usually need the services of professional groomers.

Breeds such as bull terriers and Staffordshire bull terriers were once used as fighting dogs. Fortunately, dog fighting is no longer a sport. These dogs make loving family pets, although they do not always get along well with other dogs.

Hounds

Hounds are divided into breeds that hunt by following scent trails and breeds with sharp eyes that hunt by sight.

A basset hound has long ears and a long body. Its short legs keep its body close to the ground and its nose close to the scent trail.

Many people do not want purebred dogs. Dogs with parents of different breeds (**crossbreeds**) or dogs of unknown breeding (**mongrels**) make great pets, too.

Scent hounds, which include dachshunds, beagles, and basset hounds, have a fantastic sense of smell. They like nothing better than following scent trails, and they sometimes even ignore their owners' calls.

Sight hounds, which include greyhounds, salukis, and Irish wolfhounds (the tallest breed), can run faster than any other breed. They are tall, elegant dogs with sweet tempers, but they still have strong hunting **instincts** and are not good choices for people who have cats or other small animals as pets.

Herding

Some dogs were bred to work with livestock, especially sheep and cattle. Herding breeds, such as border collies, Australian shepherds, and bearded collies, love to work and have enormous amounts of energy. These breeds need plenty of exercise and lots of training to keep their minds occupied.

Working

Because they have been used as guard dogs, many of the biggest and most impressive breeds are in the working dog category. Mastiffs (the heaviest of all breeds), Great Danes, and rottweilers are in this group. These dogs are very loyal, but, because they are so big

Rottweilers were bred to guard their homes and owners. They need experienced handlers.

and strong, they need expert training. Dogs that were bred to pull sleds, such as Siberian huskies and Alaskan malamutes, are also in this group.

Toy
Small, or toy, breeds were developed to be **lap dogs**. They include Yorkshire terriers, papillons, and Chihuahuas (the smallest of all breeds). Such little dogs do not need much exercise, but they

When fire engines were horse-drawn, dalmations ran beside the wagons because dalmations were not afraid of horses.

require a lot of coat care. Many of them are long-haired. Toy dogs are very affectionate with their owners, but some toy dogs are too delicate to live in families with small children.

Sassy, curious Chihuahuas are small dogs with big personalities!

Nonsporting
All breeds that do not fit into any other category are called nonsporting dogs. This group includes dalmatians — lively dogs with spectacular spotted coats that are the mascots of firefighters. The Boston terrier, an all-American breed, and poodles, whose curly coats need regular clipping, are also nonsporting dogs.

Getting Ready

Get ready for the new arrival before you bring a dog into your home.

A dog has simple needs, but certain items are still essential.

Food

Find out what the puppy or dog you want has been eating and get enough of that food for the first week. Packaged dog food is much better than table scraps.

Bowls

A dog needs two bowls: one for drinking water and one for food. Stainless steel bowls are the sturdiest and easiest to clean.

Training Crate

A wire crate is especially useful for a puppy. It provides a safe, secure place for the pup at night

Take time introducing your puppy to its training crate so it is happy to be inside the crate. Never use the training crate to punish a puppy.

and can be used when the owner cannot supervise the puppy. If a pup is fed in its training crate from the beginning, it will soon see the crate as a special den.

Bed

Manufactured dog beds range from bean bags to igloos. A plastic, kidney-shaped bed is the sturdiest kind. It comes in several sizes. Old blankets make cozy bedding.

Where you put a dog's bed is as important as the bed itself. Many owners find that kitchens or utility rooms work best as their dogs' bases. A new puppy may want to be closer to people the first night. Using its crate for a bed would allow the puppy to sleep in a bedroom for a while.

Collar

Most dogs wear collars all the time so getting a collar that fits well is important. An adult should be able to slide one finger easily under a collar when it is fastened around a dog's neck.

Leash

Trigger-type fastenings are the most secure and keep leashes safely attached to collars.

Toys

Dogs love to play. The more you play with your dog, the more it will see you as a special friend. Toys are also useful for puppies that need to chew. The safest toys are cotton tug toys and hard, rubber toys because they will not break or splinter.

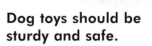

Dog toys should be sturdy and safe.

The Right Choice

With so many breeds to choose from, how do you find the best dog for your family?

Before you and your family decide which kind of dog to get, you should ask yourself these questions:

- What was the breed that you like first used for?
- How much exercise will the dog need?
- How big will the dog be when it is full grown?

- How much grooming will the dog need?
- Does this breed get along with children?
- Is the dog likely to get along with other pets?

If you want a purebred dog, you will need to go to a breeder who specializes in the breed you like. If not, you may have a friend who has a litter of puppies that need homes, or you may decide to go to an animal shelter. In all cases, the most important thing is to make sure the animal is fit and healthy. If you choose a puppy, it should be at least eight weeks old.

An older dog may need more time to get used to a new home than a puppy would.

Signs of Good Health

Before choosing a dog, make sure it is fit and healthy.

Ears
Look inside the dog's ears to see if they are clean. The ears should also smell fresh.

Eyes
Look for clean, bright eyes.

Body
The dog should not be too fat or too thin. Its body should not have any lumps, bumps, or swellings.

Nose
Crustiness around the nose is a bad sign.

Mouth
Make sure the dog's gums do not look sore and that the dog does not have bad breath.

Feet
Lift the dog's feet, one at a time, and check the pads for cracks or cuts.

Coat
Regardless of the kind of coat the dog has, check for bald patches, sore areas, and signs of dandruff.

An Older Dog?

An older dog may suit your family better than a puppy. Animal shelters have many dogs that need good homes. An older dog may find it harder to get used to a new home, at least at first. It may need expert training to fit in with its new family, but knowing that you have given a dog a second chance can be very rewarding.

Puppy Power

Puppies are so cute, you may want to take a whole litter home with you.

Puppies in a litter often look a lot alike. They may all be the same color, have similar markings, and appear equally sweet and cuddly.

To find out more about the puppies, take time to look at them closely as they run around and play. Watch how the puppies relate to each other and how the puppies' mother treats them.

Puppy Watching

When you watch the puppies, look for the following:

- **A pup that runs right out to greet you**
  This puppy is lively and confident. It may be a little bigger and stronger than the other puppies. It has no worries and will settle down quickly with its new family.

How can you figure out which is the right pup for your family?

Watch puppies play together to find out what each pup is like.

- **A pup that likes to play rough with its littermates**
  This puppy is bossy, and you will probably see its mother telling it off. A strong puppy like this will need firm handling in a new home.
- **A pup that is reluctant to come to greet you and is startled by loud noises**
  This puppy is nervous and will need careful handling to become a confident dog. It may not do well in a home with small children who might not understand why the puppy is afraid of them.
- **A pup that loves toys and rushes out to fetch any object thrown to it**
  A lively puppy like this one will love to be trained. The more you give it to do, the happier it will be. If you want to get involved in any dog sports, this puppy would be a good choice.

Male or Female?
Except for toy breeds, male dogs often grow into bigger, more powerful animals than female dogs. Sometimes, male dogs are less obedient than female dogs and need firmer handling.

Unless you intend to let your dog have puppies, you should plan on **neutering** it — an operation that prevents unwanted puppies. Neutering animals also helps them avoid several health problems, and dogs are often calmer and better behaved after neutering.

Making Friends

Dogs love people. With good care and lots of affection, you and your dog will soon be the best of pals.

When a dog first comes into your home, let the dog meet each member of the family, one at a time.

When it is your turn, talk to the dog. Tell the dog how beautiful and smart it is. Pet it and give it a treat. The dog will soon realize you are its friend. Next, try playing a game with the dog. It might like fetching toys or playing tug-of-war.

Other Family Animals

If you have other pets, you need to teach your dog to get along with them.

Dogs

If you have another dog in the family, you should let the two dogs meet outdoors so they do not feel crowded. The dogs will "talk" to each other and will make friends more quickly if they are allowed to figure out their relationship by themselves.

Most dogs are friendly and outgoing. After a game and a treat, your dog will decide that its new home is great.

Cats

Dogs love to chase anything that moves — and that includes cats. Make it clear to your dog, right away, that it must stay calm when your cat is around.

- Start off with your cat in a carrier so the dog can go up to it and sniff it without having to run after it. Call the dog to you, and then give it lots of praise, as well as a treat, when it moves away from the cat.
- Next, put the dog on a leash, and let the cat out of the carrier. Again, reward the dog with a treat when it looks at you rather than at the cat.
- When the dog has learned to be calm around the cat, you can let it off the leash.

As soon as a dog learns that chasing the family cat is not allowed, a friendship may develop.

Small Animals

If you have a small animal, such as a hamster or a guinea pig, let your dog sniff its hutch or cage. Then, call the dog away and reward it with a treat. If you repeat this a few times, your dog will soon learn that you are more interesting than the small animal in the cage, but make sure the dog is never left alone near the cage.

Paw Mark

Always play with your puppy at ground level. Do not pick it up or carry it because it could easily wriggle out of your arms and fall. If you want to hold the puppy, sit on the floor and put the pup in your lap.

Caring for a Dog

Dogs need care and attention. Figure out a good daily routine.

Dogs are classified as carnivores (meat-eaters), but they are really **omnivores**, which means they will eat anything.

correct balance of **nutrients** in their diets to stay healthy, it is better to buy food that is made specially for dogs than to feed pets table scraps.

Feeding

Adult dogs usually need two meals a day. Puppies need three a day. Because dogs need the

Grooming

The amount of grooming a dog needs depends on its coat. Short-haired dogs, such as Labrador retrievers, are the easiest to groom. Often, a weekly brushing is enough. Some breeds, such as the golden retriever, have feathered coats that need to be combed through a couple of times a week to keep tangles from forming. Long-haired breeds, such as the Afghan hound, need daily grooming.

An Old English sheepdog has a long, shaggy coat that needs a lot of grooming to keep in good shape.

This dog has learned to catch a Frisbee! This kind of playing is good fun and a great form of exercise.

Exercise

A puppy does not need much exercise. Play sessions in the backyard or short outings to the park are all it requires for the first few months. Once it is nine months old, however, it can use more exercise.

Adult dogs need regular walks. The amount of exercise a dog must have depends on its breed, its size, and its age. All dogs love to be taken out for a change of scenery and a chance to investigate new scents.

It is a good idea to take your dog out to busy places where it will see crowds of people and get used to traffic sounds. The dog will learn to accept new situations, and it will be a calm, sensible companion whenever you go out together.

Playtime

Playing with a dog is more fun than work, but it is an important part of looking after a dog. Some games also serve as exercise. Try some or all of the following games with your dog.

- Hit a ball with a tennis racquet so your dog can chase it.
- Hide behind a tree. Then call your dog so it has to find you.
- Hide a favorite toy and tell your dog to find it.

Paw Mark

All dogs must have routine health care, including worming, flea treatments, and **vaccinations**. Ask a veterinarian for advice.

Dog Behavior

Dogs do not use words, but they do have a language.

Dogs originally lived in packs, which means that understanding each other was very important. They still use their sense of smell to "read" messages left by other dogs, and they "talk" to one another using sounds and body positions.

Scent Signals

Dogs track scents, on the ground and in the air, that tell them all the local dog news. They find out who has been visiting, a male or a female, and if the female is ready for mating. When dogs meet, they greet each other by sniffing. A dog will know the members of its family by sight but also by smell.

Sound Signals

Barking: A dog has a warning bark to say that strangers are approaching. It uses a happy, excited bark when it is playing or welcoming the family home.

Whining: A dog will whine if it is unhappy or in pain.

Growling: Meant as a warning to others, growling means "Leave me alone" or "I am really fierce."

Howling: A dog's howling goes back to the days when wolves howled together to boost their team spirit before going on a hunt.

Body Language

Tail Wagging: Everyone knows that tail wagging is a sure sign of a happy dog. Some dogs also put their ears back when they wag their tails, particularly when greeting their owners.

The dog on the right is trying to make friends, but the other dog seems to want to attack.

Playing: When a dog spreads its front paws, puts its head near the ground, looks up, and wags its tail, it is inviting someone to play.

Guarding: When a dog stands completely still with its head raised and its ears forward, listening for the slightest sound, it is in a guarding position.

Cowering: A cowering dog will lower its body to the ground. Its tail will go between its legs, and it will fold its ears back. Sometimes a dog will roll onto its back to show that it is not a threat.

Looking Fierce: When it wants to look fierce, a dog will stand as tall as possible and carry its tail high over its back. Some dogs may even raise the hairs on their backs.

Attacking: A dog that is about to attack will snarl, curl its lips back, and show its teeth.

Paw Mark

When a dog is ready to take orders, it may lift its head and prick its ears. Sometimes, it will stand with a front paw raised, waiting for a command.

Training Targets

Dogs are very intelligent and can learn to do many things.

All dogs should learn basic obedience. Good training will teach a dog good manners and also help the dog understand its place in its family. Training teaches a dog to respect the leader of the family "pack."

Training does not have to be a chore. It can be fun, and you and your dog will have a rewarding relationship if you work together.

Paw Mark

Teach your dog the basics of good behavior, and then, if you like, you can move on to some tricks, such as teaching your dog to shake hands.

Reward-based Training

If you are teaching a new exercise, you want your dog to be an eager pupil. An important part of training a dog is finding a reward it really loves. For most dogs, food is the best reward, but some dogs like toys even better. Many dogs will work harder if their reward is a game played with a favorite toy.

Sit

Your dog must learn to sit so it will stay in one place for you. Teaching a dog to sit is easy. Hold a treat just above the dog's nose. As it looks up, it will sit down. When it is down, give it the treat. Repeat the lesson a few times. Then add the command "sit." In time, the dog will sit on command and will not need the treat.

Shaking Hands

Ask your dog to sit, and hold a treat just out of reach. The dog will use its paw to try to get the treat. When the dog lifts its paw, say "paw."

With practice, the dog will learn that when you hold up a treat and say "paw," it must lift its paw. Now, shake hands and reward it with the treat.

Stay

Stand facing your dog and tell it to sit. Take one step back, hold out your hand, with your palm facing the dog, and say "stay." Wait a few seconds. Then go back and reward the dog. Repeat these actions, taking more steps back each time until the dog will "stay" when you are far away.

Come

Ask a helper to hold onto your dog, and then run off and call the dog to you. Call the dog's name and say "come" in an excited voice. When the helper releases the dog, it should head straight for you. Reward the dog right away with a treat.

Heel

You want your dog to walk by your side on a loose leash, without pulling. When your dog is in the correct position at your heel, reward it with praise. If the dog tries to pull ahead, come to a standstill. With practice, the dog will learn that it is more rewarding to walk at your heel than to pull.

Glossary

allergic: likely to have a reaction to dog hair or other substances that results in health problems

ancestors: relatives from the distant past

breeding: producing an animal by mating a male and a female that have desired traits

Canidae: a large family of doglike animals

carnivores: meat-eaters

cooperating: working as a team

crossbreeds: animals with parents of different breeds

domestic: no longer living in the wild

evaporation: the process of changing water to water vapor

fossils: remains of an animal from the past, usually preserved in rock

instincts: behaviors an animal is born with

lap dogs: dogs that are small enough to fit on a person's lap

mammals: warm-blooded animals, usually covered with hair, that give birth to live young

microchip: a small electronic device

mongrels: dogs of unknown parentage

neutering: surgery that prevents an animal from reproducing

nutrients: the substances in food that keep an animal healthy

omnivores: animals that eat all kinds of foods

packs: groups of animals that live and hunt together

prey: animals that are hunted and killed by other animals, usually for food

prick: to make the ears stand straight up

purebred: describing a dog with parents that are both the same recognized breed

track: to follow a scent trail

vaccinations: injections or "shots" to protect against diseases

More Books to Read

101 Facts About Puppies
Julia Barnes
(Gareth Stevens)

**How Smart Is Your Dog?
30 Fun Science Activities
to Do with Your Pet**
D. Caroline Coile
(Sterling)

I Spy Dogs
I Spy
(Michelin Travel Publications)

**Puppytalk: 50 Ways to Make
Friends with Your Puppy**
Simon Whaley
(Hodder Children's Books)

**Totally Fun Things to Do with
Your Dog**
Maxine Rock
(Jossey-Bass)

Web Sites

American Kennel Club – Kids' Corner
www.akc.org/public_education/kids_corner/kidscorner.cfm

Dog Play: Activities for Dogs
www.dog-play.com

How to Love Your Dog
www.loveyourdog.com

Publisher's note to educators and parents: Our editors have carefully
reviewed these Web sites to ensure that they are suitable for children. Many
Web sites change frequently, however, and we cannot guarantee that a site's
future contents will continue to meet our high standards of quality and
educational value. Be advised that children should be closely supervised
whenever they access the Internet.

Index